English Version

한글
함께 배워요

Let's Learn
Hangeul *Together*

한글, 함께 배워요

발행일 2019년 11월 22일 1쇄
펴낸이 아리랑한국문화원
글·구성 이주란 번역 손경희, 민진희, 신지훈 삽화 안도현 교정 이상원 디자인 강경업
문의 070-8644-3017 E-mail jr4334@naver.com
copyright © 2019 아리랑한국문화원

발행처 상생출판 발행인 안경전 전화 070-8644-3156 팩스 0303-0799-1735
주소 대전시 중구 선화서로29번길 36(선화동) 홈페이지 www.sangsaengbooks.co.kr
출판등록 2005년 3월 11일(제175호) ISBN 979-11-90133-18-0

가격은 뒤표지에 있습니다.

이 도서의 국립중앙도서관 출판예정도서목록(CIP)은 서지정보유통지원시스템 홈페이지(http://seoji.nl.go.
kr)와 국가자료종합목록 구축시스템(http://kolis-net.nl.go.kr)에서 이용하실 수 있습니다. (CIP제어번호 :
CIP2019043564)

Beginner's Book

English Version

한글
함께 배워요

Let's Learn
Hangeul Together

◉ 손경희·이주란 저

상생출판

목차目次 Contents

1부 이치를 알면 더 재미있다!
Part One. Understanding the principles makes the learning more enjoyable!

2부 우리는 한글을 배워요.
Part Two. Let's Learn Hangeul Together – Reading & Writing

부록 Appendix ────────────────────

책을 펴내며

'한글 배우기'는 한국어를 익히기 위한 첫걸음이다.

왜냐하면, 한국어를 표현하기 위한 도구 즉 한국의 공식 문자가 '한글'이기 때문이다.

한국과 한국 문화에 관심이 많은 학습자도 한국어를 배우는 것이 의욕만큼 쉽지 않다고 말하는 경우가 종종 있다. 그러나 한국의 문자인 한글 자체는 누구나 쉽게 배울 수 있다. 아마 여러분은 그 이유를 이 책을 통해 곧 알게 될 것이다.

이 책 『한글, 함께 배워요』에서는 한글의 자음과 모음 글자를 익히기 전에, 한글을 배우는 데 도움이 되는 몇 가지를 먼저 제시했다. 한국은 어떤 나라이며, 한글을 창제한 세종대왕은 어떤 분이신지, 또 세종대왕이 한글을 만드신 원리는 무엇인지를 여러분과 함께 알아볼 것이다.

그 부분이 바로 〈이치를 알면 더 재미있다!〉이다.

〈이치를 알면 더 재미있다!〉는 한글을 배우기 위한 예비적 단계이다. 마치 한국어라는 세계로 여행을 떠나기 위해 멋지게 채비하는 것과 같다. 어떤 일을 할 때 준비를 잘하면 좋은 결과를 얻을 확률이 높듯이, 여러분이 이 단계를 제대로 알고 즐기면 한글 배우기가 한층 쉬울 것이다.

그래서 저자는 여기에 한글 탄생의 문화적인 배경과 정보를 많이 담으려고 노력했다. 모든 학습자가 재미있게 즐기기를 바란다.

이 책 『한글, 함께 배워요』의 학습을 마친 사람은 한국어 공부를 본격적으로 할 수 있는 완벽한 준비를 하게 될 것이다.

행운을 빈다!

Preface

Learning the Korean alphabet, Hangeul, is considered as the first step in learning the Korean language. One first needs to know the official writing system of Korea, Hangeul, in order to learn how to write and speak in Korean. Even those who have a strong interest in Korea and its culture often report their difficulty in learning Korean. However, learning the Korean alphabet itself isn't very challenging. You will soon find the reason through this book.

Before starting practical learning sessions on consonants and vowels of Hangeul, this book, Let's Learn Hangeul Together, introduces a few things that can help your understanding of Hangeul: facts and symbols of Korea and about the King Sejong, the inventor of Hangeul, as well as the principles applied to the constitution of Hangeul alphabets. The featured chapter, The deeper you understand, the more fun you'll have, contains all these stories.

This featured section, <Understanding the principles makes learning more enjoyable!>, is like a preliminary step in learning Hangeul. I'm sure that studying this section well will prepare you for a trip to the world of the Korean language. Just as good preparation for a certain job guarantees good results on the job, this will help you learn Hangeul more easily. I tried to provide as much cultural background information as possible, particularly about the creation of Hangul. I hope you will enjoy reading those pages.

Those who study using this book will find themselves prepared for learning the Korean language. I wish you all the best of luck!

1
부

Part One

1 한국과 한국어
Korea and Its Language

1) 세계 속의 한국Korea in the World

🇰🇷 **한국은 아시아의 북동쪽 끝, 중국과 일본 사이에 위치한다.**
Korea is located at the far end of Northeast Asia between China and Japan.

한반도 전체는 동경 124~132도, 북위 33~43도에 있다. 남북한 전체 면적은 221,000㎢이며, 그중 남한 땅은 45%이다. 면적의 크기로 보면, 남한은 세계 약 250여 개 국가 중에서 백 아홉째이다. 북쪽을 제외한 삼면이 바다로 둘러싸여 있다.

우즈베키스탄, 터키, 이탈리아, 모로코, 스페인 등은 그 위도가 한국과 비슷하고, 필리핀, 인도네시아, 오스트레일리아 등은 같은 경도상에 위치한다.

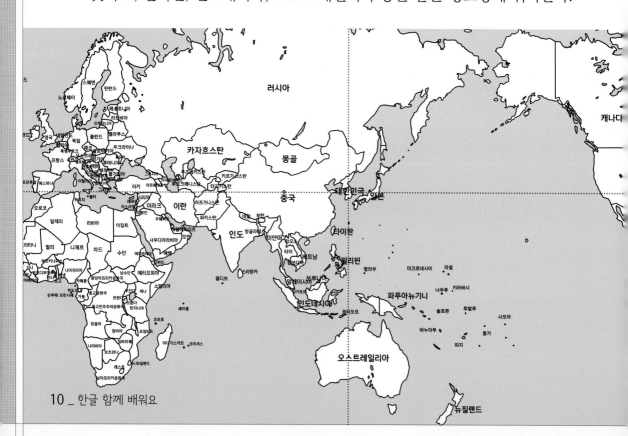

과테말라, 아이슬란드, 헝가리, 포르투갈 등은 그 면적이 남한과 비슷하다.

한국은 중국과 일본 사이에 위치한다. 고대부터 세 나라 사이에는 문화 교류가 있었으며, 서로 영향을 주고받았다. 그 속에서 각자의 독특한 문화를 계승, 발전시켜 왔다.

The entire Korean Peninsula is located between 124 and 132 degrees east longitude and 33 and 43 degrees north latitude. The total area of the two Koreas is 221,000 square kilometers, 45% of which is South Korea. South Korea is the 109th out of about 250 countries in the world in terms of its size. Three sides of the country, except the northern side, are surrounded by the seas.

The latitude of Uzbekistan, Turkey, Italy, Morocco, and Spain is similar to that of Korea, while the Philippines, Indonesia, and Australia are located on the equivalent longitude. Guatemala, Iceland, Hungary, and Portugal are similar to South Korea in terms of size.

Korea is located between China and Japan. There have been numerous cultural exchanges between the three countries since the ancient times. In the heart of mutual influences, each country has inherited and developed its own unique culture.

한국의 국호는 '대한민국'이다.
Korea's official name is the Republic of Korea.

월드컵 경기에서 한국을 응원하며 터져 나왔던 함성, '대~한민국 짝짝짝짝짝', 방탄소년단(BTS)이 노래와 춤을 통해 알리는 나라, 한국의 공식 명칭이 바로 '대한민국'이다. 앞에서 언급한 '남한'을 가리켜 대한민국이라 한다.

1897년 10월 12일 조선 왕조의 마지막 왕 고종은 국호를 '조선'에서 '대한제국'으로 바꾸었다. '환구단'을 지어 천지에 제사를 올리고 대한제국 황제에 오르는 의식을 행하였다. 고종 황제는 대한제국을 열강과 동등한 자주 국가로 만들고자 했으나 뜻을 이루지 못하였다.

1910년 8월, 일본이 한일병합조약을 통해 대한제국의 국권을 빼앗아 버렸다.

그 후 국내외에서 항일독립운동이 전개되었다. 1919년 3월 1일에는 전국적인 독립만세 운동이 일어났다. 이를 계기로 1919년 4월 13일 중국 상하이에 대한민국 임시정부가 수립되었다. 그때 '대한민국'을 국호로 정하였다.

1945년 8월 15일, 일본이 연합국에 항복하자 한국인들은 광복을 맞이하였다.

1948년 8월 15일, 대한민국 정부 수립이 선포되었다.

You might be familiar with this cheering cadence "Dae~hanminkuk, clap-clap-clap-clap-clap!," chanted by the Red Devil, supporters of the Korean national soccer team. If not, you may have heard of BTS, a world-famous boy band from South Korea. Do you know how Korean people call their own country? They call it "Daehanminkuk."

On October 12th, 1897, King Gojong, the last ruler of the Joseon Dynasty, changed the country's name from 'Joseon' to 'the Korean Empire'. He built the royal altar called 'Hwangudan' and there enthroned himself as the first emperor of the empire, performing a ritual honoring heaven and earth. Emperor Gojong tried to develop his empire and proclaim it as an independent state, having equal right to other imperial countries of great power. Unfortunately, he did not succeed in actualizing his vision.

The sovereignty of the Korean empire was taken away by Imperial Japan in August 1910. The annexation ignited anti-Japanese independence movements both locally and abroad. In particular, the nationwide movement that took place on March 1st 1919 helped establish the Korean Provisional Government in Shanghai, China, on April 13th, 1919. This is when they gave their country the new name, the 'Republic of Korea.'

Korea reclaimed its independence simultaneously with Imperial Japan's surrender to Allied Forces on August 15th 1945. The establishment of the Korean government was proclaimed on August 15th in 1948.

환구단 Hwangudan

삼일절(3.1절)
Independence Movement Day (Samiljeol)

한국의 국경일이다.

1919년 3월 1일, 한국인들이 일본의 식민통치에 항거하는 독립선언서를 발표하였다. 그때 '대한독립 만세'를 부르며 독립 의지를 세계에 알린 것을 기념하는 날이다.

1919년 3월 1일 당시 민족대표 33인이 한국의 독립을 선언한 '3·1 독립선언서'를 발표했다.

2019년은 3·1 독립 만세 운동이 일어난 지 100년이 되는 해이다.

It is the official national holiday in South Korea.

On March 1st, 1919, Koreans issued the Declaration of Independence against the Japanese colonial rule.

This day commemorates the Koreans who then proclaimed to the whole world their will to independence by shouting "Long Live Korean Independence!"

On that day, 33 Korean leaders issued the March First Declaration of Independence, which proclaimed the independent statehood of Korea.

The year 2019 marks the 100th anniversary of the March 1st Independence Movement.

ㅎ 대한민국의 국기는 '태극기'이다.

The national flag of Korea is Taegeukgi

원래 태극기에는 팔괘가 그려져 있었다. 그런데 고종이 역관 오경석이 올린 태극과 사괘의 도안을 사용하면서 건곤감리 사괘가 그려진 태극기가 되었다.[1] 1882년 8월 박영효 일행이 일본으로 타고 간 메이지마루 호에 태극과 사괘를 그린 태극기가 게양되었다는 것은 잘 알려진 사실이다. 이후 1883년에 태극기는 한국의 정식 국기가 되었다.

흰 바탕에 태극 문양을 가운데 두고 네 모서리에 사괘를 그린 태극기는 19세기 말에 만들어졌다. 그러나 태극기에 그려진 태극 문양은 고대부터 우리 생활 곳곳에 사용되었다.

동양 우주론에서 천지 만물은 음과 양이라는 생명력을 바탕으로 존재하고 변화해 간다고 본다. 태극은 음양이 나뉘기 전의 상태이다. 음과 양이 하나로 역동하는 모습을 나타낸다. 건곤감리 사괘는 천지일월(건 – 하늘, 곤 – 땅, 감 – 달/물[水], 리 – 해/불[火])을 의미한다.

태극기의 바탕은 흰색이다. 빛의 삼원색은 빨강, 초록, 파랑이다. 이 모두를 합치면 흰색이 된다. 그래서 흰색은 빛을 상징한다. '빛'은 '밝음'을 의미하며, 모든 생명을 살아 숨 쉬게 하는 원동력이다. 이처럼 한국의 국기인 태극기에는 동양 우주론과 철학적 원리가 담겨 있다.

Originally, Taegeukgi, the national flag of Korea, had eight trigrams painted on its white background. Later on, Emperor Gojong ordered that it be changed into one having a *Taegeuk* (or Taiji) symbol at the center and four surrounding trigrams, as suggested by the royal translator, Kyeong-seok Oh. It is well known that Taegeukgi was first raised on the ship *Meiji Maru* in August 1882, when

---

1) 『나는 박물관 간다』, 상생출판, 2018, 214쪽
『I Am Going To the Museum』, Sangsaeng Books, 2018, p.214

the royal court's official Young-hyo Park and his companions boarded the ship to travel to Japan. In 1883, Taegeukgi became the official flag of Korea.

The current and typical design of Taegeukgi, which has the *Taegeuk* symbol in its center and the four trigrams placed at the corners, was made in Korea during the late 19th century. However, the symbol of *Taegeuk* had been used everywhere in the daily lives of Korean people since ancient times.

According to the Eastern philosophy on the universe, all life on earth exists and undergoes numerous changes in accordance with the dynamic movement of the two coexistent vital energies called yin and yang. The symbol of *Taegeuk* signifies the very state of oneness of these two vitals, yin and yang, in which they are not separated from each other; it represents the two dynamics acting and coexisting as one. The four trigrams at the corners stand for heaven, earth, sun/fire, and moon/water.

Taegeukgi's background color is white. Combining the three primary colors of "light"-- red, green, and blue-- creates a white color. Therefore, the white color symbolizes "light." The "light" means "brightness," as the fundamental source for all living creatures to stay alive. This is the essence of Eastern philosophy and cosmology that we can learn from the principles embodied within Taegeukgi.

ㅎ **통계로 본 한국** (출처: 국가통계포털)

Statistics about South Korea (Source: KOSIS)

인구(Population) : 51,811,167 (as of 2019)

경제활동인구(Working population) : 28,216,000 (as of 2019)

고령인구 비율(Elderly population rate) : 14.9% (as of 2019)

합계출산율(Birth rate) : 1.052 per family (as of 2017)

기대수명(Life expectancy) : 82.7 years (as of 2017)

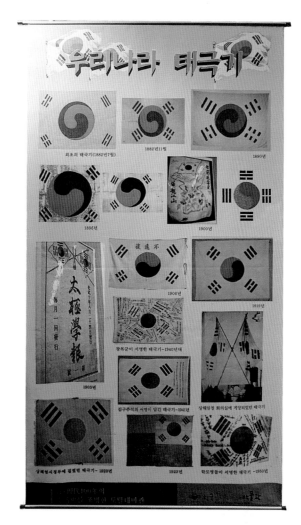

태극기 - 파주 근현대사 박물관
Taegeukgi - The Museum of
Modern History of Korea in Paju.

생활 속에서
사용된 태극
Taegeuk designs
in dailylife

'한韓'은 무슨 뜻일까요?
What does the word '한(Han;韓)' mean?

한국인은 스스로 '대한 사람'이라 하고 자기 민족을 '한민족'이라 부른다. 한국인이 입는 고유한 옷을 '한복', 먹는 음식을 '한식', 살던 집을 '한옥'이라 한다. 국외에서 유행하는 한국의 대중문화도 '한'자를 붙여 '한류'라 한다.

'한'을 국어사전에서 찾아보면 여러 뜻으로 풀이한다.

① 하나 ② 대략 ③ 같다 ④ 어떤, 어느 ⑤ 하다의 관형사형으로 큰, 많은 ⑥ 바르다 ⑦ 한창 ⑧ 가득하다 ⑨ 한韓 : 나라 이름 / 성姓의 하나 등의 의미를 지닌다.[2]

이외에도 '중앙[가운데]'을 나타내기도 하고, 역사적으로 '임금'을 뜻하는 말로도 쓰였다. 나아가 '광명'이라는 뜻도 있다.

Koreans call themselves '*Daehan-saram* (대한사람)'. They use the word '*Hanminjok* (한민족)', which means '*Han* race,' referring to their ethnicity. The words *Hanbok*, *Hansik*, and *Hanok*, refer to traditional Korean clothes, food, and houses, respectively. Of course, *Hallyu*(한류), the Korean cultural wave, has the word '한(韓)' in its writing.

The word "*Han* (한)" has various meanings as follow:

(1) one, as a number　　　　　(2) approximately

(3) to be the same

(4) in the same sense of the indefinite articles, a or an

(5) to be large, to be many or much of something

(6) to be right or righteous　　(7) at one's fullest of something

(8) to be abundant　　　　　(9) a country name or a surname

In addition to these meanings, "*Han*" also means the "middle", "center", or a "king" in a historical context. "Brightness" or "radiance" is also included in the meanings of the word '*Han*'.

---

2) 『민중 에센스 국어사전』, 민중서림, 4판, 이희승 감수
『Minjung Essence Korean Dictionary』, Minjung Seorim Publishing, 4th Edition, Edited by Hee-seung Lee

역사와 문화를 통합해서 본다면, '한'의 으뜸 정신은 밝음을 지향하는 '광명'이라 말할 수 있다. 광명 즉 '빛'은 우주 만물의 실상이며 본성으로서 한국인의 조상들은 하늘의 광명을 '환桓', 땅의 광명을 '단檀'이라 하고 이 하늘과 땅 의 광명을 실현하는 역사의 주인공을 '한'이라 했다. 그래서 하나이면서도 크다는 의미를 기본적으로 담아서 나라 이름을 한없이 세상을 비추는 빛이 될 '대한'이라 한 것이다.[3]

이에 대해, 한철학과 한사상을 연구한 김상일 교수는 '<한>의 어원을 찾아보면 <한>은 단순히 추상적인 개념이 아니고 한국인들의 실존Korean Existence이요 생물적인 본능에서 우러나온 말'이라고 정의했다.[4]

From an overall historical and cultural perspective, the most significant meaning among them is 'brightness.' Brightness or radiance is the reality and the true nature of all existence in the universe. According to Korean historical texts, ancient Koreans referred to the radiance of heaven as "*hwan*", and the radiance of earth as "*dan*". The leaders who realized the dreams and ideals of the Heaven and Earth in the world were called "*Han*". Having this word "*Han*(한)", meaning "one and great" at the same time, Korean ancestors gave their country the promising name "Daehan(대한)", in the hope that their nation will benefit and illuminate the entire world.

A renowned scholar Kim Sang-il, who studied the Han philosophy and ideology, traced the origin of 'Han' and defined the word 'Han' as the 'Korean Existence', which originated from the biological nature of Koreans, instead of a mere abstract concept.

---

3) 한민족을 때로는 배달민족, 배달겨레라 일컫기도 하는데, 배달이라는 국명도 '밝은 땅'을 의미한다.
The Korean nation is occasionally referred to as Baedal nation or Baedal Gyeorae. Here, the state name of Baedal signifies the bright land.
4) 『한철학』, 상생출판, 김상일, 2014, 36쪽
『The Philosophy of Korea』, Sangsaeng Books, Sang-il Kim, 2014, p.36

2) 한국어 The Korean language

ㅎ 한국인이 사용하는 공식적인 언어이다.

Korean is the official language that Koreans use.

ㅎ 세계에서 한국어는 얼마나 사용하고 있을까요?

How many people in the world speak Korean?

ㅎ 한국어는 국제특허협력조약(PCT)에서 국제공개어로 지정된 언어이다.[5] 한국어로 국제 특허를 출원하거나 특허 내용을 열람할 수 있다.

Korean is one of the official languages of publication in the regulations under the Patent Cooperation Treaty (PCT). An international patent can be filed in Korean; Korean translation is also provided when accessing patent documents.

---

5) 국제특허협력조약에서 처음 지정한 공개언어는 영어, 프랑스어, 독일어, 일본어, 러시아어, 스페인어, 중국어, 아랍어 등 8개였으나, 2007년 한국어와 포르투갈어가 추가되었다.

At first, eight languages such as English, French, German, Japanese, Russian, Spanish, Chinese, Arabic were designated as official languages by Patent Cooperation Treaty. Later, in 2007, Korean and Portuguese were included.

2 세종대왕과 한글
Sejong the Great and Hangeul(the Korean Alphabet)

1) 세종대왕은 누구인가?Who is Sejong the Great?

세종대왕[6]은 조선 시대(1392~1910)[7] 넷째 임금이다.

Sejong the Great was the fourth king of the Joseon Dynasty.

1397년, 아버지인 태종과 어머니 원경왕후 민 씨의 셋째 아들로 태어났다.
재위 기간은 1418년부터 1450년까지 32년간이다.

He was born as the third son to King Taejong and Queen Wongyeong in 1397 and his reign lasted for 32 years, from 1418 to 1450.

1443년에 훈민정음을 만들었다. 3년 후인 1446년에 반포했다.

Sejong the Great invented Hunminjeongeum (Hangeul) in 1443. After three years of testing, he promulgated it in 1446.

한국의 만 원권 지폐에 세종대왕 초상이 들어있다.

The Korean bill for 10,000 won shows the portrait of Sejong the Great printed on its front side.

---

6) 한국인들은 위대한 업적을 남긴 세종을 흔히 세종대왕이라 부른다. '대왕'은 '위대한 왕'이라는 뜻이다.
Koreans usually call him King Sejong the Great, honoring his great contribution. Daewang means Great King.
7) 조선은 고려 이후 개국된 나라이다. 조선을 세운 태조 이성계는 한양(지금의 서울)을 수도로 삼았다.
Joseon was the nation that succeeded Goryeo. The founder of Joseon Dynasty Taejo Seong-gye Yi made Hanyang (modern-day Seoul) the capital city.

유네스코 세종대왕 문해상
UNESCO King Sejong Literacy Prize

유네스코에서는 세계 각국에서 문맹 퇴치에 공헌한 개인이나 단체 두 곳을 뽑아 해마다 상을 수여한다. 그 상의 이름은 '유네스코 세종대왕 문해상'이다.

이 상은 세종대왕의 한글 창제 정신을 전 세계에 알리고, 지구촌에 문해 교육을 촉진하기 위한 것이다. 대한민국 정부의 지원으로 1989년에 제정되어 1990년부터 매년 시상하고 있다.

UNESCO annually awards the "UNESCO King Sejong Literacy Prize" to two institutions or individuals for their contribution to eliminating illiteracy.

This prize was established in 1989 with the support of the Korean government. It is aimed at widely spreading King Sejong's spirit of Hangeul invention and promoting literacy in the world.

2) 한글과 훈민정음 Hangeul and the Hunminjeongeum

🈎 한글은 한국어를 표기하는 공식 문자이다.

Hangeul is the official writing system to transcribe the spoken Korean language.

🈎 훈민정음은 한글의 옛 이름이다.

Hunminjeongeum is the original name of Hangeul.

세종대왕 때 새 문자를 만든 목적과 원리를 밝힌 책 이름이기도 하다.

'한글'이라는 이름은 주시경[8] 선생이 붙였다. 1910년 이후 '한글'이라는 명칭이 널리 퍼졌다.[9]

It also refers to the book that Sejong the Great published, explaining the purpose of creating the new writing system and its forming principles.

The current name 'Hangeul' was coined by Ju Si-gyeong, a Korean linguist. It became widely known among the public after 1910.

🈎 훈민정음은 '백성을 가르치기 위한 바른 소리'라는 뜻이다.

Hunminjeongeum means "correct sounds for instructing the people."

조선 시대에는 훈민정음을 '정음 28자'라고 하였는데, 주로 '언문'이라 불렀다.

During the Joseon Dynasty, Hunminjeongeum was called "Jeongeum 28 letters," or more commonly known as "Eonmun."

---

8) 주시경(1876~1914)은 한글 학자이자 독립 운동가이다. 한국어 문법의 기초를 놓은 분이라 할 수 있다.

Si-gyeong Ju(1876-1914) was a scholar of Hangeul and independence activist. He built a foundation for the grammar of Korean language.

9) 『훈민정음 해례본』, 교보문고, 김슬옹, 37쪽

『Hunminjeongeum Manuscript』, Gyobo Book Center, Seul-ong Kim, p.37

🏛 한글이 만들어지기 전에는 지식인층을 중심으로 한자를 썼다.

It was not until Sejong the Great invented Hunminjeongeum that the most common people of Joseon were able to write their own opinions and thoughts using the new script.

그런데 일반인은 대부분 그들의 생각을 글로 표현할 수 없었다.

세종대왕이 훈민정음을 만든 이후 일반인도 자신이 뜻하는 바를 문자로 나타 낼 수 있었다.

Before the invention of Hangeul, only a limited number of people, particularly the elite, used Chinese characters to transcribe their spoken Korean language.

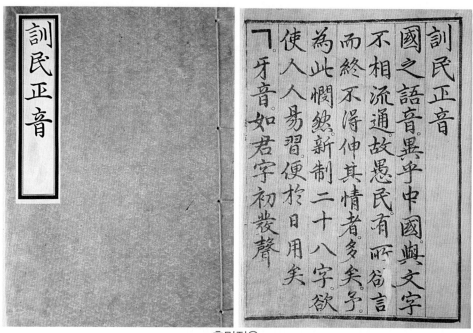

훈민정음
Hunminjeongeum

《〈훈민정음〉》 해례본은 어떤 책인가?
What kind of book is «Hunminjeongeum Haerye»?

세종대왕은 훈민정음을 만들고, 훈민정음의 원리와 사용법을 알려주는 《〈훈민정음〉》을 펴냈다. 흔히 《〈훈민정음〉》 해례본이라고 부른다.

Sejong the Great created the new script "Hunminjeongeum" and published the commentary 《Hunminjeongeum》, or 《Hunminjeongeum Haerye》 as a more popular name, to reveal the principles and usage of the letters.

🔘 표지를 제외하고 총 66쪽으로 이루어졌다.

The book consists of 66 pages, excluding the cover page.

🔘 내용은 세종대왕이 쓴 '예의편(정음)'과 신하들이 쓴 해례편 (정음해례)으로 크게 나눌 수 있다.

The commentary Hunminjeongeum Haerye can be divided into two major sections. The first section is called Yeuipyeon or Jeongeum (section of examples and definitions), which was authored by King Sejong; the second section is called Haeryepyeon or Jeongeumhaerye (Section of explanations and examples), which was authored by his collaborating scholars.

《〈훈민정음〉》 해례본 《Hunminjeongeum Haerye》			
정음편 Jeongeum		정음해례편 Jeongeumhaerye	
어제(세종) 서문 The preface by King Sejong	예의편 Yeuipyeon (Examples and Definitions)	해례편 Haeryepyeon (Explanations and Examples)	정인지 서문 The preface by Jeong In-ji

1446년에 훈민정음을 반포할 때, 기본 글자는 28자였다.
자음 17자와 모음 11자이다.

When it was promulgated in 1446, Hunminjeongeum consisted of 28 basic letters, including 17 consonants and 11 vowels.

ㄱ	ㄴ	ㄷ	ㄹ	ㅁ	ㅂ	ㅅ	ㅇ	ㅈ	ㅊ	ㅋ	ㅌ	ㅍ	ㅎ
ㆆ	ㆁ	ㅿ	ㆍ	ㅏ	ㅑ	ㅓ	ㅕ	ㅗ	ㅛ	ㅜ	ㅠ	ㅡ	ㅣ

현재 한글의 기본 자모는 24자이다.
사용하지 않는 네 글자 : 자음 'ㆁ(옛이응), ㆆ(여린히읗), ㅿ(반시옷)', 모음 · (아래아)

The modern Korean alphabet is comprised of 24 letters.
The four letters, ㆁ, ㆆ, ㅿ, ㆍ, are obsolete nowadays.

1962년, 대한민국 국보 제70호로 지정되었으며 1997년에는 유네스코 세계기록 유산으로 등재되었다.

Hunminjeongeum Haerye was designated as Korean national treasure No. 70 in 1962 and was listed as a UNESCO Memory of the World Register in 1997.

3 한글의 제자 원리
The principle of Hangeul formation

1) 한글은 기본 자음 14자와 모음 10자로, 모두 24자이다.

이 자음과 모음이 확장되어 자음 21자와 모음 19자가 쓰인다. 모두 40자로 이루어져 있다.

Today, Hangeul consists of 24 basic letters, including 14 consonants and 10 vowels. These basic letters were expanded to 21 consonants and 19 vowels by combination and variation of the letters. This is why we now have 40 orthographic Hangeul letters.

2) 한글에는 동양의 천지인 삼재 사상과 음양오행의 이치가 담겨 있다.

The Korean writing system, 'Hangeul,' embraces the Eastern philosophy of the 'Three Fundamentals of the Heaven, Earth, and Human', the principle of Yin,Yang, and the Five Elements.

<<훈민정음>>의 정음해례편에는 다음과 같은 설명이 나온다.

"천지자연의 이치는 오로지 음양오행뿐이다. …

정음 28자는 각각 그 모양을 본떠서 만들었다. …

무릇 사람의 말소리는 오행에 뿌리를 두고 있다. 그러므로 사계절에 합하여도 어그러짐이 없으며, 오음과 맞추어 봐도 잘 어울리고 틀리지 않는다. … 중성은 하늘, 땅과 사람에서 본뜬 것을 취하니, 천지인 삼재의 이치를 갖추었다."

《Hunminjeongeum Haerye》 explains it as follows.

"The Yin, Yang, and the Five Elements is the one and only principle that propels changes in heaven and earth. …

The 28 letters were formulated according to the principle of Yin-Yang and the Five Elements. ...

The articulation of the oral sounds of humans happens based on the principle of the Five Elements. There is neither disaccord with the principle of four seasons, nor disharmony with the five musical sounds of gung, sang, gak, chi, and u. Jungseong, the medial sounds, symbolize the Three Fundamentals of the Heaven, Earth, and Human.”

3) 자음은 발음 기관의 모양을 본떠서 만들었다.

The consonants were designed after the shapes of articulatory organs at the moment of pronunciation.

기본자 Basic Consonants					
	ㄱ	ㄴ	ㅁ	ㅅ	ㅇ
	어금닛소리 Molar sound	혓소리 Lingual sound	입술소리 Labial sound	잇소리 Dental sound	목구멍소리 Glottal sound

가획 글자 / 병서자 Extended Consonants					
	ㅋ	ㄷ, ㅌ	ㅂ, ㅍ	ㅈ, ㅊ	ㅎ
	ㄲ	ㄸ	ㅃ	ㅆ, ㅉ	

* ㄹ : 반혓소리 글자. 혀의 모습을 본떴으나 가획하지는 않음.
불청불탁음.
ㄹ is a semi-lingual sound which is modeled after the shape of tongue, with no strokes added. The ‘ㄹ’ sound is neither clear nor voiced.

4) 모음은 천지인 삼재인 하늘, 땅, 사람을 본떠서 ㆍ, ㅡ, ㅣ 를 만들고, 이 글자를 바탕으로 다른 모음 글자를 만들었다.

The three basic vowels(ㆍ, ㅡ, ㅣ) were invented in unison with the principle of the 'Three Fundamentals of the Heaven, Earth, and Human,' and were developed to make the rest of the vowels.

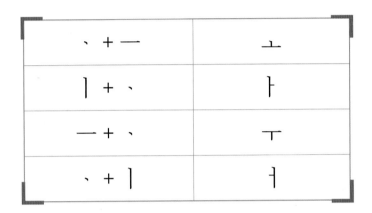

천지인을 적용한 자판
The mobile phone keypad using the method called *cheon-ji-in*,
meaning *heaven-earth-human*

5) 한글은 자음과 모음을 모아써서 하나의 음절을 이룬다.

In the Hangeul transcription system, one consonant and one vowel are combined to constitute one syllable.

🖸 하나의 음절은 초성, 중성, 종성으로 되어 있다.
One syllable consists of initial, medial, and final sounds

초성과 종성에는 자음을 쓰고, 중성에는 모음을 쓴다.

하나의 음절이 초성, 중성, 종성이 모두 갖추어졌을 때, 종성을 흔히 '받침' 이라 부른다.

The initial and final sounds are expressed by the consonants, and the medial sounds, by the vowels. When one syllable has all three different sound units, the trailing consonant sound is referred to as 'Batchim'.

🖸 모음만으로 이루어진 음절은 첫 자음의 자리에 소리 없는 'ㅇ'을 붙인다.
Syllables that begin with a vowel have 'o', the silent consonant, to fill the space.

자음 + 모음 a consonant + a vowel	예 : ㄱ + ㅏ	가
소리 없는 'ㅇ'+ 모음 silent 'o' + a vowel	예 : ㅇ + ㅏ	아
자음 + 모음 + 자음(받침) a consonant + a vowel + a consonant(*Batchim*)	예 : ㄱ + ㅏ + ㄱ	각
소리 없는 'ㅇ'+ 모음 + 자음(받침) silent 'o' + a vowel + a consonant(*Batchim*)	예 : ㅇ + ㅏ + ㄴ 예 : ㅇ + ㅗ + ㄱ	안 옥

6) 하나의 음절은 왼쪽에서 오른쪽으로, 위에서 아래의 순서로 쓴다.

The Hangeul characters are written from left to right, and from top to bottom.

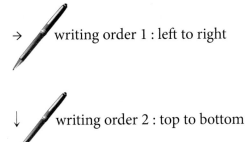

→ writing order 1 : left to right

↓ writing order 2 : top to bottom

음양오행 이치와 훈민정음
Yin-Yang, Five Elements and Hunminjeongeum

'음양'이란 인간과 만물이 생겨나고 유지되게 하는 서로 다른 성질의 생명 기운이다. 밝고 따뜻한 성질인 '양'이 있고 어둡고 차가운 성질인 '음'이 존재한다. 우주 삼라만상이 음양의 이치에 따라 변화한다.

그런데 훈민정음에도 음양의 이치가 그대로 들어있다.

ㅡ(땅) 위에 . (하늘)를 놓으면 ㅗ가 된다. 이것은 밝은 소리이므로 양이다. ㅡ(땅) 아래에 . (하늘)를 놓으면 ㅜ가 된다. 이것은 어두운 소리이므로 음이다. (하늘)를 ㅣ(사람)밖에 놓으면 ㅏ가 되는데 이것은 양이다. (하늘)이 ㅣ(사람)안에 놓이면 ㅓ가 되는데, 이것은 음이다.

오늘날 한국어에서 의성어나 의태어뿐 아니라 단어들을 자세히 보면 양성 모음은 양성 모음끼리 음성 모음은 음성 모음끼리 어울리는 경향을 볼 수 있다.

오행이란 다섯 오五, 갈 행行 자로 만물을 낳고 기르는 다섯 가지 기운을 말한다. 음양을 세분화한 것으로 이해하면 된다. 다만 오행에는 음과 양 이외에, 서로 다른 기운을 조화롭게 하는 '토' 기운이 있다는 것이 특징이다.

다섯 가지 기운은 목(木), 화(火), 토(土), 금(金), 수(水)이다. 이것은 달력에서도 볼 수 있다.

나무(목)	봄 ⋯⋯⋯⋯⋯⋯	ㄱ
불(화)	여름 ⋯⋯⋯⋯⋯	ㄴ
흙(토)	늦여름 ⋯⋯⋯⋯	ㅁ
쇠(금)	가을 ⋯⋯⋯⋯⋯	ㅅ
물(수)	겨울 ⋯⋯⋯⋯⋯	ㅇ

세종대왕은 이러한 자연의 이치 즉 음양오행을 훈민정음에도 고스란히 적용하였다.

Yin and *yang* is life energy with distinct nature that allows human beings and all existence on earth to come into being and be maintained. *Yang* energy is bright and warm, while *yin* energy is dark and cold. All things in the universe change according to the Yin-yang principle. Hunminjeongeum also embraces this principle of *yin* and *yang* in its writing system.

The vowel 'ㅗ' is made when '·'(the Heaven) is put on 'ㅡ'(the Earth). This vowel 'ㅗ' is a bright sound or a sound with *yang* quality. On the other hand, '·'(the Heaven) is put under 'ㅡ'(the Earth) to create a dark sound or a sound of *yin* quality, 'ㅜ'. In the same manner, the point '·'(the Heaven) can be placed to the left or right side of 'ㅣ'(the Human) to form 'ㅓ', a dark sound, or 'ㅏ', a bright sound, respectively.

In the modern Korean usage, there is a tendency for vowels with *yang* quality go with other yang vowels, and for vowels with *yin* quality to go with other yin vowels. This is observable not only in mimetic words or onomatopoeia, but also in common words.

The Five Elements refer to the five different energy forms that give birth to and nurture all life in the universe. The Sino-Korean word meaning the Five Elements is 五行(*o-haeng*), which is made up of '五'(five) and '行'(process). The Five Elements are wood, fire, earth, metal, and water, four of which were derived and diversified from *yin* and *yang*. Among these energy forms, it is the *earth* energy that balances and harmonizes the rest of the energy forms. The Five Elements can also be seen in the calendar system.

Wood	Spring	ㄱ
Fire	Summer	ㄴ
Earth	Indian summer	ㅁ
Metal	Autumn	ㅅ
Water	Winter	ㅇ

Sejong the Great applied the principles of nature, particularly the principle of *yin* and *yang* and the Five Elements, into the invention of Hunminjeongeum.

한글을 나라의 공식 문자로 선포한 사람은 누구일까요?
Who declared Hangeul as the official script of the country?

그분은 바로 고종(1852 – 1919)임금으로, 조선의 제26대 왕이자 대한제국 초대 황제이다.

고종은 1894년 11월 21일에 칙령을 내려 한글을 나라의 공식 문자로 선포하였다. 이것은 세종대왕이 훈민정음을 창제한 지 450여 년이 흐른 뒤였다. 그때까지도 한글은 위치는 여전히 두 번째였다.

왜냐하면, 훈민정음이 반포된 이후에도 한자가 첫 번째 공식 문자의 역할을 하였기 때문이다.

고종은 나라의 위상을 바로잡기 위해 개혁을 단행하였다. 그 중에서 어문정책으로 '법률과 칙령은 모두 국문國文으로 기본을 삼되, 한문 번역을 덧붙이거나 국문과 한문을 혼용한다.'고 규정하였다.

이로써 비로소 한글이 공식적으로 '나라의 문자'가 되었다.

이 칙령에 따라 한글로 쓴 첫 공문서는 1895년 1월 고종이 발표한 개혁 강령인 '홍범 14조'이다.

It is King Gojong (1852–1919), the 26th king of Joseon and the first emperor of the Korean Empire.

Gojong issued a decree on November 21st, 1894, proclaiming Hangul as the official script of the country. This was 450 years after King Sejong's completion of Hunminjeongeum. Until then, Sino-Korean characters had served as the first official script, whereas Hangeul had to stay in the second place even after its promulgation.

King Gojong implemented reforms to improve the status of his country. Among them, the royal decree on literacy stipulated that both laws and edicts must be written in Hangeul, with translations to Sino-Korean script or the combined form of Hangeul and the Sino-Korean script only when necessary.

Through this royal announcement, Hangul officially became the national script of Korea. The first official document written in Hangul under this decree was the reformative legal norms, the Hongbeom 14 Articles of the Guiding Principles for the Nation, promulgated by King Gojong in January 1895.

고종 황제가 승하한 곳은 지금의 덕수궁이다.
덕수궁의 본래 이름은 경운궁이다.
덕수궁의 함녕전을 찾아가 보는 것도 뜻깊은 일일 것이다.

The residence where Emperor Gojong lived his last days and passed away was the Deoksugung Palace.

The original name of the palace was Gyeongungung.

It would be meaningful to visit the Hamnyeongjeon Hall of Deoksugung Palace.

덕수궁 전경
Deoksugung Palace in its entirety

함녕전
Hamnyeongjeon Hall

한글 자모의 이해
Understanding the Consonants and Vowels of Hangeul

1) 기본 자음 14자 The Fourteen Basic Consonants

ㄱ	ㄴ	ㄷ	ㄹ	ㅁ	ㅂ	ㅅ
기역 giyeok	니은 nieun	디귿 digeut	리을 lieul	미음 mieum	비읍 bieup	시옷 Siot
ㅇ	ㅈ	ㅊ	ㅋ	ㅌ	ㅍ	ㅎ
이응 ieung	지읒 jieut	치읓 chieut	키읔 kieuk	티읕 tieut	피읖 pieup	히읗 hieut

2) 단모음 10자 The Ten Basic Vowels : Monophthongs

ㅏ	ㅓ	ㅗ	ㅜ	ㅡ	ㅣ	ㅐ	ㅔ	ㅚ	ㅟ
아 a	어 eo	오 o	우 u	으 eu	이 i	애 ae	에 e	외 oe	위 wi

> ☑ 'ㅐ'와 'ㅔ'의 소리는 원래 다르지만, 현재는 거의 같게 발음한다.
>
> The pronunciations of the two vowels ㅐ and ㅔ were originally different from each other. However, modern Korean native speakers mostly pronounce these two vowels the same way.

3) 쌍자음 5자 The Five Double Consonants

ㄲ	ㄸ	ㅃ	ㅆ	ㅉ
쌍기역 ssang-giyeok	쌍디귿 ssang-digeut	쌍비읍 ssang-bieup	쌍시옷 ssang-siot	쌍지읒 ssang-jieut

4) 이중모음 11자 The Eleven Compound Vowels : Diphthongs

ㅑ	ㅕ	ㅛ	ㅠ	ㅒ
야 ya	여 yeo	요 yo	유 yu	얘 yae

ㅖ	ㅘ	ㅙ	ㅝ	ㅞ	ㅢ
예 ye	와 wa	왜 wae	워 wo	웨 we	의 ui

🗣 '왜', '외'와 '웨'의 소리도 원래 다르지만, 외국인분만 아니라 한국인도 구별하기 어렵다. 거의 같게 발음한다.

The pronunciations of the three vowels - ㅙ, ㅚ, and ㅞ - were originally different from each other. However, even Korean native speakers, not to mention foreign speakers, can hardly distinguish them from one another. There is essentially no difference in pronunciations of these three vowels nowadays.

5

알아둘 표현
Useful Expressions

책을 펴세요.	Open your book.
책을 보세요.	Look at your book.
잘 들으세요.	Listen carefully.
따라 하세요.	Repeat after me.
크게 읽으세요.	Read it out loud.
쓰세요.	Write the words.

◉ 답을 고르세요.	Choose the correct answer.
◉ 함께 해 보세요.	Try it together.
◉ 시작해 볼까요?	Shall we begin?
◉ 수업을 마칠게요.	That is all for today.
◉ 질문 있어요?	Do you have any questions?

2
부

Part Two

우리는 한글을 배워요.
Let's Learn Hangeul Together –
Reading & Writing

1과

학습목표 Learning Objective
모음 글자 1 익히기
Monophthongs

---

1. 들어보세요.
Listen carefully.

---

2. 단모음 10자 읽고 써 봅시다.
Let's read out loud and copy the ten basic vowels, monophthongs below.

모양 shape	쓰기 순서 writing order		따라 쓰기 copy	
ㅏ		아		
ㅓ		어		
ㅗ		오		
ㅜ		우		
ㅡ		으		
ㅣ		이		
ㅐ		애		
ㅔ		에		
ㅚ		외		
ㅟ		위		

듣고 고르세요.
Listen to the sound and select the matching character.

1　① 아　　② 어　　**2**　① 어　　② 오

3　① 아　　② 우　　**4**　① 오　　② 우

5　① 으　　② 어　　**6**　① 이　　② 으

듣고 따라 하세요.
Listen and repeat after the speaker.

1　아　　이　　우　　에　　오

2　아　　우　　오　　우　　이

3　으　　이　　으　　이　　우

4　어　　아　　우　　어　　애

단어를 읽고 써 봅시다.
Read the words out loud and copy them.

오이			
아이			
에이			

듣고 글자를 써 보세요. 교사는 앞에서 배운 모음 중
두 글자를 조합하여 들려준다.

Listen carefully to the sounds and write the matching characters.
The teacher presents the combinations of two characters from the vowels
they had learned earlier.

* 아오, 어우, 이외, 으와

❶

❷

❸

❹

연습
5

(짝 혹은
팀 활동) 카드의 글자를 친구에게 귓속말로 전달하세요.
마지막 전달받은 사람이 칠판에 글자를 씁니다.

Whisper the characters on the card to your neighbor.
The last person should write the characters on the board.

학습목표 Learning Objective
자음 글자1 익히기
Consonants 1

1. 들어보세요.
Listen carefully.

2. 자음 글자 읽고 쓰기
Let's read out loud and write consonants.

ㅎ 자음 글자의 각각의 이름은 있으나 홀로 발음되지 않는다.
Consonants can't be pronounced alone even though they have their own names.

모양 shape	쓰기 순서 writing order	따라 쓰기 copy		
ㄱ	ㄱ	ㄱ		
ㄴ	ㄴ	ㄴ		
ㄷ	ㄷ	ㄷ		
ㄹ	ㄹ	ㄹ		
ㅁ	ㅁ	ㅁ		
ㅂ	ㅂ	ㅂ		
ㅅ	ㅅ	ㅅ		
ㅇ	ㅇ	ㅇ		
ㅈ	ㅈ	ㅈ		

호 모음 글자와 자음 글자를 함께 써 봅시다.

Let's practice combining vowels and consonants.

	ㅏ	ㅓ	ㅗ	ㅜ	ㅡ	ㅣ	ㅐ	ㅔ	ㅚ	ㅟ
ㄱ	가	거	고	구	그	기	개	게	괴	귀
ㄴ	나	너	노	누	느	니	내	네	뇌	뉘
ㄷ	다	더	도	두	드	디	대	데	되	뒤
ㄹ	라	리	로	루	르	리	래	레	뢰	뤼
ㅁ	마	머	모	무	므	미	매	메	뫼	뮈
ㅂ	바	버	보	부	브	비	배	베	뵈	뷔
ㅅ	사	서	소	수	스	시	새	세	쇠	쉬
ㅇ	아	어	오	우	으	이	애	에	외	위
ㅈ	자	저	조	주	즈	지	재	제	죄	쥐

호 'ㄱ'은 모음의 결합에 따라 모양이 조금 달라진다.

The shape of 'ㄱ' slightly changes according to the connecting vowels.

호 'ㅇ'에 모음이 결합한 모습과 앞에서 배운 단모음 10자의 쓰기 모양이 같다.

The shapes of vowels combined with 'ㅇ' are similar to the written forms of the ten basic vowels.

	ㅏ	ㅓ	ㅗ	ㅜ	ㅡ	ㅣ	ㅐ	ㅔ	ㅚ	ㅟ
ㄱ										
ㄴ										
ㄷ										
ㄹ										
ㅁ										
ㅂ										
ㅅ										
ㅇ										
ㅈ										

듣고 고르세요.

Listen to the sound and select the matching character.

1 ① 고   ② 거   **2** ① 바   ② 버

3 ① 도   ② 드   **4** ① 스   ② 즈

5 ① 지   ② 디   **6** ① 구   ② 부

7 ① 시   ② 지

연습
2

듣고 고르세요.

Listen to the sound and select the matching words.

1 ① 자다   ② 사다   **2** ① 고이   ② 구이

3 ① 주스   ② 소스   **4** ① 에그   ② 개그

단어를 읽고 써 봅시다.
Read the words out loud and copy them.

나	나			
너	너			
어머니	어머니			
아버지	아버지			
누나	누나			
나라	나라			
모자	모자			
다리	다리			
지우개	지우개			
소리	소리			
가위	가위			
바지	바지			
배게	배게			

듣고 쓰세요.

Listen carefully to the sounds and write the matching characters.

❶

❷

❸

❹

❺

❻

❼

쉬어가기 Take a Break

호 인사해 봅시다.

Let's greet one another.

감사와 사과
Thanking and Apologizing

모음 글자 2 익히기
Diphthongs

1. 들어보세요.
Listen carefully.

2. 이중모음 11자 읽고 쓰기
Let's read out loud and copy the 11 diphthongs below.

모양 shape	쓰기 순서 writing order		따라 쓰기 copy		
ㅑ		야			
ㅕ		여			
ㅛ		요			
ㅠ		유			
ㅢ		의			
ㅒ		얘			
ㅖ		예			
ㅙ		왜			
ㅞ		웨			
ㅝ		워			
ㅘ		와			

ⓗ '㏚'와 '㏔'를 거의 같게 발음하듯이, 'ㅒ'와 'ㅖ'의 발음도 원래 같지 않지만, 현재는 거의 같게 발음한다.

Just as 'ㅐ' and 'ㅔ' sound alike, 'ㅒ' and 'ㅖ' are currently pronounced almost the same way. However, they were originally pronounced differently.

ⓗ 앞에서 이미 설명했지만 'ㅙ', 'ㅚ'와 'ㅞ'의 발음도 원래 같지 않지만, 외국인분만 아니라 한국인도 구별하기 어렵다. 거의 같게 발음한다.

'ㅙ', 'ㅚ' and 'ㅞ' were originally different just like the case for 'ㅐ' and 'ㅔ'. It is not easy even for native Korean speakers to distinguish one from the other, for their pronunciations are almost the same.

ⓗ 모음 글자와 자음 글자를 함께 써 봅시다.

Let's practice combining vowels and consonants.

	ㅑ	ㅕ	ㅛ	ㅠ	ㅢ	ㅒ	ㅖ	ㅙ	ㅞ	ㅝ	ㅘ
ㄱ	갸	겨	교	규	긔	걔	계	괘	궤	궈	과
ㄴ	냐	녀	뇨	뉴	늬	냬	녜	놰	눼	눠	놔
ㄷ	댜	뎌	됴	듀	듸	댸	뎨	돼	뒈	둬	돠
ㄹ	랴	려	료	류	릐	럐	례	뢔	뤠	뤄	롸
ㅁ	먀	며	묘	뮤	믜	먜	몌	뫠	뭬	뭐	뫄
ㅂ	뱌	벼	뵤	뷰	븨	배	볘	봬	뷔	붜	봐
ㅅ	샤	셔	쇼	슈	싀	섀	셰	쇄	쉐	숴	솨
ㅇ	야	여	요	유	의	얘	예	왜	웨	워	와
ㅈ	쟈	져	죠	쥬	즤	쟤	졔	좨	줴	줘	좌

	ㅑ	ㅕ	ㅛ	ㅠ	ㅢ	ㅒ	ㅖ	ㅙ	ㅞ	ㅝ	ㅘ
ㄱ											
ㄴ											
ㄷ											
ㄹ											
ㅁ											
ㅂ											
ㅅ											
ㅇ											
ㅈ											

듣고 고르세요.

Listen to the sound and select the matching character.

❶ ① 와 　② 의 　③ 워

❷ ① 갸 　② 규 　③ 교

❸ ① 쥬 　② 쥐 　③ 줘

❹ ① 려 　② 례 　③ 류

❺ ① 과 　② 괘 　③ 계

연습 2

읽고 쓰세요.

Read the words out loud and copy them.

우유	우유		
여유	여유		
아우	아우		
여우	여우		
예의	예의		

읽고 쓰세요.

Read the words out loud and copy them.

사과	사과			
교수	교수			
과자	과자			
돼지	돼지			
의사	의사			
샤워	샤워			
스웨터	스웨터			
시계	시계			
세계	세계			
요리사	요리사			
교과서	교과서			

연습 4 1과에서 3과까지 배운 글자들이 들어간 단어를 사전에서 찾아 쓰세요. (10개 찾기)

In your Korean dictionary, please find and write 10 words that have the characters that you learned from Lesson 1 through Lesson 3.

❶

❷

❸

❹

❺

❻

❼

❽

❾

❿

쉬어가기 Take a Break

ㅎ 일부터 십까지 숫자를 배워 봅시다.

Let's learn numbers from 1 to 10.

ㅎ 한국인이 가장 좋아하는 숫자는 무엇일까요?

Which number do you think Koreans like the most?

숫자 Number	발음 Pronunciation
1	일
2	이
3	삼
4	사
5	오
6	육
7	칠
8	팔
9	구
10	십

자음 글자2 익히기
consonants 2

1. 들어보세요.
Listen carefully.

2. 모음 글자와 자음 글자를 함께 써 봅시다.
Let's practice combining vowels and consonants.

순서	ㅏ	ㅑ	ㅓ	ㅕ	ㅗ	ㅛ	ㅜ	ㅠ	ㅡ	ㅣ
ㅋ										
ㅌ										
ㅍ										
ㅊ										
ㅎ										

3. 다음을 비교해서 발음해 봅시다. 무엇이 달라요?
Pronounce the following consonant pairs and compare them.
How are they different?

❶ ㄱ → ㅋ   ❷ ㅂ → ㅍ

❸ ㄷ → ㅌ   ❹ ㅈ → ㅊ

듣고 고르세요.
Listen to the sound and select the matching word.

① ① 가위 ② 키위   **②** ① 자리 ② 차리

③ ① 포도 ② 보도   **④** ① 후주 ② 후추

⑤ ① 다음 ② 타음

'아이우에오와외'와 '하히후헤호화회'를 발음해 봅시다.
Pronounce the following sets: '아이우에오와외' and '하히후헤호화회'

아 이 우 에 오 와 외

하 히 후 헤 호 화 회

읽고 쓰세요.
Read the words out loud and copy them.

코	코		
귀	귀		
커피	커피		
치마	치마		
우표	우표		
포도	포도		
채소	채소		
회사	회사		
휴지	휴지		
피아노	피아노		
카메라	카메라		
도토리	도토리		
티셔츠	티셔츠		

한국어 자음 체계표 Phonetic Charts for Korean Consonants

		양순 Bilabial	치경 Alveolar	치경 구개음 Alveolo-palatal	연구개 Velar	성문 Glottal
파열음 Plosive	평음 Lax	ㅂ	ㄷ		ㄱ	
	경음 Tense	ㅃ	ㄸ			
	격음 Aspirated	ㅍ	ㅌ			
마찰음 Fricative	평음 Lax		ㅅ			ㅎ
	경음 Tense		ㅆ			
	격음 Aspirated					
파찰음 Affricate	평음 Lax				ㅈ	
	경음 Tense				ㅉ	
	격음 Aspirated				ㅊ	
비음 Nasal		ㅁ	ㄴ		ㅇ	
유음 Liquid			ㄹ			

학습목표 Learning Objective

자음 글자 3 익히기
consonants 3

---

1. 들어보세요.
Listen carefully.

---

2. 다음을 발음해 봅시다.
Let's pronounce the characters below.

평음 (예사소리) Lax Consonants	경음 (된소리) Tense consonants	격음 (거센소리) Aspirated consonants
가	까	카
버	뻐	퍼
소	쏘	
두	뚜	투
자	짜	차

연습 1

듣고 고르세요.
Listen to the sound and select the matching character.

1 ① 고 　　② 꼬　　　**2** ① 뚜 　　② 두

3 ① 써 　　② 서　　　**4** ① 자 　　② 짜

5 ① 빼 　　② 배

연습 2

듣고 고르세요.
Listen to the sound and select the matching character.

1 ① 파 　　② 바　　　**2** ① 주 　　② 추

3 ① 그 　　② 크

연습 3

듣고 고르세요.
Listen to the sound and select the matching character.

1 ① 고 　　② 코　　　**2** ① 바 　　② 파

3 ① 사 　　② 싸　　　**4** ① 부 　② 푸 　③ 뿌

5 ① 다 　② 타 　③ 따　　**6** ① 과 　② 콰 　③ 꽈

7 ① 자 　② 차 　③ 짜　　**8** ① 바 　② 파 　③ 빠

읽고 쓰세요.

Read the words out loud and copy them.

토끼	토끼			
찌개	찌개			
까마귀	까마귀			
쓰레기	쓰레기			
오빠	오빠			
빠르다	빠르다			
싸다	싸다			
짜다	짜다			

다양한 글씨체|Various styles of handwriting

한글 함께 배워요

한글 함께 배워요

Hangeul

한글

한글

Han geul

한글

한글

한글

한글

Hangeul

한글, 함께 배워요

한글, 함께 배워요

한글, 함께 배워요

한글, 함께 배워요

한글, 함께 배워요

한글, 함께 배워요

한글, 함께 배워요

한글, 함께 배워요

학습목표 Learning Objective

받침 익히기1
Batchim 1

---

1. 받침 Batchim: Final Consonants(Trailing Consonant)

🗣 '자음 + 모음 + 자음'에서 마지막 자음을 받침이라고 한다.
In the 'C + V + C' combination, the final consonants are called *'Batchim'*.

각	간	갈	감	갑	갓	강

🗣 받침의 종류
Two types of Batchim

홑받침 Single Batchim

ㄱ, ㄴ, ㄷ, ㄹ, ㅁ, ㅂ, ㅅ, ㅇ, ㅈ, ㅊ, ㅋ, ㅌ, ㅍ, ㅎ, ㄲ, ㅆ

('ㄸ, ㅃ, ㅉ' 은 받침으로 사용하지 않는다.)
'ㄸ, ㅃ, ㅉ' are not used as *Batchim*.

겹받침 Double Batchim

ㄳ, ㄵ, ㄶ, ㄺ, ㄻ, ㄼ, ㄽ, ㄾ, ㄿ ㅀ, ㅄ

학습1) 듣고 맞는 받침을 고르세요.

Listen to the sound and select the Batchim that matches the sound.

① **가**   ① ㅇ   ② ㅁ

② **도**   ① ㄴ   ② ㅇ

③ **수수** ① ㄹ   ② ㄴ

④ **벼**   ① ㅇ   ② ㄹ

2. 받침 글자의 발음 Pronunciation of final consonants

🔊 받침은 'ㄱ, ㄴ, ㄷ, ㄹ, ㅁ, ㅂ, ㅇ' 7개의 대표음으로만 발음된다.

There are only seven representative sounds, 'ㄱ, ㄴ, ㄷ, ㄹ, ㅁ, ㅂ, ㅇ' when you read Batchim.

받침 Batchim	발음 Pronunciation
ㄱ, ㅋ, (ㄲ)	ㄱ
ㄴ	ㄴ
ㄷ, ㅌ, ㅅ, ㅆ, ㅈ, ㅊ	ㄷ
ㄹ	ㄹ
ㅁ	ㅁ
ㅂ, ㅍ	ㅂ
ㅇ	ㅇ

발음해 봅시다.
Pronounce the following words.

낟, 낱, 낫, 낮, 낯

'압'과 '앞'

받침의 소리가 같은 것들을 고르세요.
Encircle all the characters with the same sound Batchim.

곧	앗	앞	앉
밖	꽃	밭	숲
밥	옷	부엌	막

쓰세요.
Copy the following words.

책	책			
꽃	꽃			
빵	빵			
형	형			
언니	언니			
동생	동생			
과일	과일			
한국	한국			
김치	김치			
식당	식당			
춥다	춥다			
덥다	덥다			

호 **몸** Body

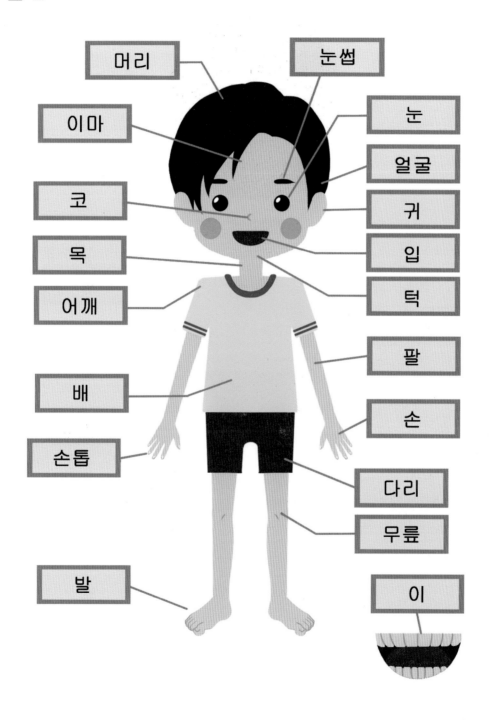

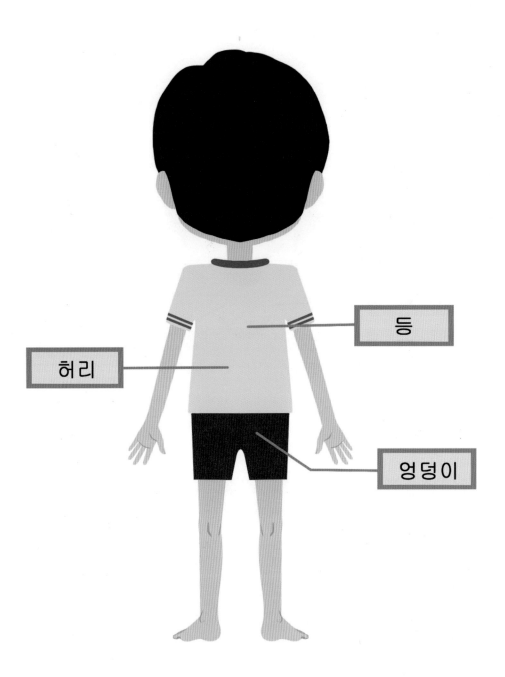

등

허리

엉덩이

7과

학습목표 Learning Objective

받침 익히기2
Batchim 2

1. 어떻게 읽을까요? How do you pronounce the following words?

구분	발음 Pronunciation
닭	[ ]
흙	[ ]
넋	[ ]
값	[ ]
삶	[ ]

🗣 겹받침은 두 개의 글자가 합하여져 이루어진 받침이지만, 실제로 발음할 때에는 둘 중의 하나만 발음된다.

Double Batchim is composed of two consonants, but only one of them is pronounced.

ㄳ	⇨	ㄱ	ㄺ	⇨	ㄱ
ㄵ	⇨	ㄴ	ㄻ	⇨	ㅁ
ㄼ, ㄽ, ㄾ	⇨	ㄹ	ㄿ	⇨	ㅍ
ㅄ	⇨	ㅂ	* 예외도 있다. There are some exceptions.		

쓰세요.
Copy the following words.

넋	넋			
앉다	앉다			
여덟	여덟			
외곬	외곬			
핥다	핥다			
값	값			
않다	않다			
싫다	싫다			
닭	닭			
삶	삶			
읊다	읊다			

ㅎ 겹받침 바로 뒤 음절이 자음으로 시작할 때 그 자음은 된소리가 된다.

The initial consonant following a double Batchim becomes tense.

- 예외) 'ㄹㄱ'이 대표음 [ㄱ]이 아닌 [ㄹ]로 나는 경우

Exception : When 'ㄹㄱ' is not pronounced as [ㄱ], but as [ㄹ].

- 예외) '발을 밟다'에서 '밟다'의 경우, 겹받침 'ㄹㅂ'이 [ㄹ]로 나지 않고 [ㅂ]이 된다.

Exception : When 'ㄹㅂ' of '밟다' is pronounced as [ㅂ], instead of [ㄹ].

연습 1

받침의 발음이 다른 것을 고르세요.

Select the word whose final consonant is pronounced differently from the rest.

1　① 읊고　　② 없다　　③ 밟지　　④ 넓고

2　① 맑게　　② 흙　　③ 맑다　　④ 늙지

3　① 여덟　　② 읽기　　③ 핥다　　④ 넓게

연습 2

발음이 맞는 것을 고르세요.

Select the number that shows the correct pronunciation.

1　밖이 매우 밝다

　① 박기 매우 발따
　② 바끼 매우 박따
　③ 바기 매우 박따

2　앉지 말고 서서 먹다

　① 안지 말고 서서 먹다
　② 안찌 말고 서서 먹따
　③ 안지 말고 서서 먹따

3　물이 많아서 갈 수가 없다

　① 물이 만아서 갈 수가 업다
　② 무리 만하서 갈 수가 업따
　③ 무리 만아서 갈 수가 업다
　④ 무리 마나서 갈 수가 업따

부록

Appendix

부록1 Appendix 1
더 배우기 : 연음
In-depth Study : Linked Sounds

ㅎ 받침 글자 뒤에 모음으로 시작되는 음절이 올 때 받침이 그 음절의
첫소리에서 발음된다.

In case the syllable starting with a vowel comes after a letter with Batchim,
the Batchim is pronounced at the initial sound of the syllable.

| 쓰기
writing | ...... | 국어 | 닭이 |
| 발음
pronunciation | ...... | 구거 | 달기 |

ㅎ 홑받침 뒤에 모음이 오는 경우를 알아봅시다.

Let's take a look at cases where a vowel follows a single Batchim.

국이 [구기]	간이 [가니]	걷어 [거더]	걸어 [거러]
감아 [가마]	밥이 [바비]	옷이 [오시]	강이 [강이]
낮에 [나제]	빛에 [비체]	부엌에 [부어케]	같아요 [가타요]
갚아 [가파]	좋아요 [조아요]	밖이 [바끼]	있어요 [이써요]

- 한국어의 'ㅇ'은 초성에서는 소릿값이 없고 종성에서만 소리 난다. 즉 연음이 일어나지 않는다.

'ㅇ' is not pronounced as an initial sound. It is pronounced only as a final sound. In other words, there is no linking process between the two 'ㅇ's.

종이	[종이] - 0	[조이] - ×
콩을	[콩을] - 0	[코을] - ×

- 받침 'ㅎ'는 연음되지 못하고 탈락한다.

'ㅎ' as a final consonant drops and is not linked to the connecting vowel sound.

놓아요	[노아요] - 0	[노하요] - ×
낳아	[나아] - 0	[나하] - ×

ㅎ 겹받침 뒤에 모음이 오는 경우를 알아봅시다.

Let's take a look at cases where a vowel comes after a double Batchim.

맑아 [말가]	앉아 [안자]	곬이 [골시] → [골씨]
삶아 [살마]	넓어 [널버]	넋이 → [넉시] → [넉씨]
핥아 [할타]	읊어 [을퍼]	없어요 [업서요] → [업써요]
있어요 [이써요]	많아요 [마나요]	싫어 → [시러]

– 겹받침의 두 번째 자음 글자가 'ㅎ'인 경우에는 연음되지 않고
  탈락한다.

'ㅎ' as the second consonant of double Batchim drops and is not linked to
the connecting vowel.

연습 1 연음이 일어나는 예를 고르세요.
Select the example where linking process occurs.

1 ① 밥도　　② 밥과　　③ 밥이　　④ 밥만

2 ① 말하며　② 길게　　③ 울고　　④ 앞에서

연습 2 연음이 일어나지 않는 예를 고르세요.
Select the example where linking process does not occur.

1 ① 콩을　　② 말을　　③ 삶을　　④ 읽을

2 ① 많아　　② 닿아　　③ 싫어　　④ 핥아

부록2 Appendix 2
한글 관련 사이트
Hangeul-related websites

국립국어원
The National Institute of the Korean Language

www.korean.go.kr

국립한글박물관
National Hangeul Museum

www.hangeul.go.kr

세종학당재단
King Sejong Institute Foundation

www.ksif.or.kr

한글학회
The Korean Language Society (Hangeul Hakhoe)

www.hangeul.or.kr

세종대왕기념사업회
Sejong the Great Memorial Foundation

www.sejongkorea.org

국제한국어교육학회
The International Association for Korean Language Education

www.iakle.com

세종대왕 연보
Sejong the Great: Chronology

참조: 세종대왕기념사업회 홈페이지
Reference: Sejong the Great Memorial Foundation website

April 10, 1397	한양의 준수방俊秀坊에서 태종의 셋째 아들로 탄생. Sejong was born as the third son of King Taejong in Junsubang, Hanyang present-day Seoul.
February 1408	충녕군忠寧君에 책봉되고, 우부대언右副代言 심온沈溫의 따님과 혼인. Sejong was officially titled Prince Chungnyong-gun, and married to a daughter of Si-mon沈溫, Ubudaeeon or Right Assistant Transmitter.
May 1412	충녕대군大君에 진봉됨. Sejong assumed the title of Grand Prince Chungnyeong-daegun.
October 1414	충녕대군의 장자인 향珦이 한양의 사저私邸에서 탄생함. Yi Hyang, the eldest son of Sejong, was born at his private residence in Hanyang.
September 1417	충녕대군의 둘째 아들인 유瑈가 본궁本宮에서 탄생함. Yi Yu, the second son of Sejong, was born at the main palace本宮.
June 1418	태종이 세자 제禔를 폐하여 양녕대군讓寧大君으로 봉하고, 충녕대군을 세자로 책봉함. 세자의 자字를 원정元正이라 함. King Taejong demoted Crown Prince, Yi Je, to Grand Prince Yangnyong-daegun, promoting Grand Prince Chungnyeong-daegun to Crown Prince. Sejong adopted Wonjeong as his adult name.
August 10, 1418	태종이 세자 충녕대군[世宗]에게 양위함. Crown Prince Chungnyeong-daegun (Sejong) ascended to the throne after Taejong's abdication.

September 1418	세종의 셋째 아들 용瑢이 탄생. 창덕궁昌德宮으로 이어移御. The third son of Sejong, Yi Yong, was born. Sejong moved to Changdeokgung Palace.
October 1418	첫 경연을 열고, ≪대학연의大學衍義≫를 강론. Sejong first established the Royal Lecture, where he expounded the *Daehak Yeonui*, or the Abundant Meanings of the Great Learning.
November 1418	전국의 의부義夫·절부節婦·효자孝子·순손順孫을 찾게 함. Sejong issued a decree that righteous men, virtuous women, filial children, and filial grandchildren be sought out throughout the country.
June 1419	삼군도체찰사三軍都體察使 이종무李從茂가 227척의 병선을 이끌고 대마도를 정벌. Yi Jong-mu, Samgun dochechalsa, or the Supreme Leader of Three Armies, conquered Tsushima Island using a fleet of 227 warships.
November 1419	전국의 사찰 노비를 혁파. Sejong ordered the abolition of the practice of slavery prevalent in Buddhist temples across the nation.
January 1420	왕자 구璆가 탄생. 전국의 효자孝子·절부節婦·의부義夫·순손順孫을 찾아 표창. The prince Gu(璆) was born. He gave commendation to righteous men(義夫), virtuous women(節婦), filial sons(孝子), and devoted grandsons(順孫) across the country.
March 1420	집현전集賢殿을 확장하여 영전사·대제학·제학·부제학·직제학 등의 녹관祿官을 둠. Sejong established government offices receiving a stipend such as Yeongjeonsa, Daejehak, Jehak, Bujehak, and Jikjehak by expanding and reorganizing Jiphyeonjeon(集賢殿) (or Hall of Worthies).
July 1420	세종의 어머니 원경왕후元敬王后 세상을 떠남. Sejong's mother, Queen Wonkyong(元敬王后), passed away.

October 1420	활자 경자자庚子字를 만들기 시작. 수군도절제사水軍都節制使를 수군도안무처치사水軍都安撫處置使로 고침. Sejong started making bronze typeface, called the Gyeongja font (; Gyeongjaja; 庚子字). He renamed the naval forces from Sugundojeoljesa(水軍都節制使) to Sugundoanmucheochisa(水軍都安撫處置使).
March 1421	주자소鑄字所에서 경자자를 완성하고 인쇄법을 개량함. 서적書籍을 중외中外에서 사들이게 함. Sejong completed a new font called Gyeongjaja at the printing office, Jujaso(鑄字所), and improved the printing process. He bought books from China and overseas nations.
June 1421	신장訊杖의 제도를 정하여 태장笞杖을 마구 못 치게 함. Sejong reformed the criminal justice system(; the penal system used a rod for official beatings; 訊杖) to regulate the punishment system of harsh striking to the body.
September 1421	원자元子의 이름을 향珦이라고 명함. Sejong named his firstborn son Hyang(珦).
October 1421	원자 향珦(文宗)을 세자로 책봉. The firstborn son of the king, Hyang(珦, 文宗) was proclaimed crown prince.
December 1421	사죄삼복계死罪三覆啓의 법을 정하여 죄인의 억울함을 적게 함. Sejong reformed the laws and regulations on the administration of major criminal cases, such as murder and high treason, which is called Sajoesamboggye(死罪三覆啓), to emphasize the importance of thorough investigation and informed judgment, in order that the victim might not suffer injustice.
May 1422	태종이 연화방蓮花坊 신궁新宮에서 승하함. King Sejong's father Taejong passed away at the residence of the king, Yyeonhwabang(蓮花坊).
September 1423	조선통보朝鮮通寶를 주조하게 함. Sejong worked on the casting of brass coins (with a square hole in the middle), called Joseontongbo(朝鮮通寶).

November 1424	변계량卜季良에게 본국의 지지地志와 주부군현의 고금 연혁을 편찬하게 함. 악기도감樂器都監에서 악기를 제조함. Byeongyelyang(卜季良) compiled the geography of home country and the history of all ages of all the local administrative districts (such as the state, the county, and the prefecture). He produced musical instruments at Aggidogam(樂器都監), the government office that was temporarily established to take charge of musical instruments in the Joseon Dynasty.
February 1425	처음으로 동전銅錢을 사용. 악서樂書를 찬집하게 하고, 악기와 악보법을 그리고 써서 책을 만들게 함. The bronze coin(銅錢) was used for the first time. Sejong compiled music documents and published a book of musical instruments and musical notations.
September 1425	예조에 단군 사당을 별도로 세우고 신위를 남향하여 제사하게 명함. Sejong ordered the Ministry of Ceremonies, Yejo, to set up a separate shrine for Dangun and conduct an offering ritual with an altar facing towards the south.
October 1426	경복궁 각 문과 다리의 이름을 정함. Sejong named each gate and bridge of the Gyeongbokgung Palace.
December 1426	젊은 학자를 뽑아 사가독서賜暇讀書하게 함. Sejong selected young and talented scholars and granted them special leave for intensive periods of study in a quiet place (such as at home or quiet Buddhist temples in the mountains).
July 1428	처음으로 종학을 세워 대군大君이나 종실宗室의 자제들로 하여금 나아가서 배우게 함. Sejong set up the first royal institute, Jonghag, for the education of children from the royal family.
May 1429	정초鄭招 등이 ≪농사직설農事直說≫을 편찬함. Jeong Cho(鄭招) and others published «Nongsajigseol(農事直說); a Plain Guide to Farming».
July 1429	신라·고구려·백제 시조묘始祖廟를 사전祀典에 기재記載하고 치제致祭하게 함. Sejong listed the ancestral shrine(始祖廟) of Silla, Goguryeo, Baekje in the ritual codes(祀典) and conducted offering rituals.

February 1430	≪농사직설農事直說≫을 반포. Sejong distributed «Nongsajigseol(農事直說); a Plain Guide to Farming».
October 1430	공처노비公處奴婢 산아産兒 휴가에 대한 법을 제정하게 함. Sejong enacted a law on maternity leave for public slaves.
June 1432	설순偰循 등이 ≪삼강행실도三綱行實圖≫를 편찬 완료함. Seolsoon(偰循) and others completed the compilation of ≪Samganghaengsildo(三綱行實圖); an Illustrated Guide to the Three Bonds≫.
July 1438	공법貢法을 경상·전라도에 시험을 행하게 함. The land tax system(; a flat-sum system of taxation; 貢法) was conducted on a trial basis in the Jeolla and Gyeongsang province.
July 1439	성주星州와 전주全州에 사고史庫를 두게 함. Sejong placed historical archives(史庫) in Jeonju (全州) and Seongju (星州).
March 1440	성혼기成婚期를 정해서 남자 16세, 여자 14세 이상으로 함. Sejong set the marriage age (成婚期) at 14 for women and 16 for men.
August 1441	측우기測雨器를 제작 비치함. Sejong invented and installed a rain gauge, called Chugugi(測雨器).
December 1443	훈민정음訓民正音 28자를 창제. Sejong invented 28 letters of the Korean alphabet, Hangeul, Hunminjeongum(訓民正音).
February 1444	훈민정음으로 운회韻會를 번역하게 함. 최만리崔萬理 등이 훈민정음의 반대 상소를 함. Sejong had Woonhoe(韻會) translated using Hunminjeongum. Choi Man-Ri(崔萬理) and others made an appeal against Hunminjeongum.
January 1445	신숙주·성삼문成三問·손수산孫壽山을 요동遼東에 보내어 운서韻書를 질문하여 오게 함. Sejong sent his scholars (Shin Seung-Ju, Seong san-moon, Son soo-san(孫壽山)) to Liaodong(遼東), China to ask about Yunseo(韻書).

April 1445	권제權踶 등이 ≪용비어천가龍飛御天歌≫ 10권을 지음. Kwon Je(权踶) and others authored 10 books of ≪Yongbi Ochonga(龍飛御天歌); the Songs of Flying Dragons≫.
March 1446	왕비王妃 소헌왕후昭憲王后가 수양대군首陽大君 제택第宅에서 승하함. Queen Soheon(昭憲王后) passed away at the residence of Suyangdaegun(首陽大君).
September 1446	훈민정음을 반포함. ≪훈민정음(해례본)≫이 이루어짐. Sejong promulgated Hunminjeongum(; the Proper Sounds for Istructing the People). ≪Hunminjeongum (Haeryebon; original copy)≫ was published together with a commentary.
November 1446	언문청諺文廳을 설치. Sejong installed Eonmuncheong(諺文廳), which is the government office in the royal court for compilation and printing of books after the creation of Hunminjeongeum.
December 1446	이과吏科 및 이전吏典 시험에 훈민정음을 시험 과목에 넣음. Sejong included Hunminjeongeum as an examination subject for Igwa(吏科) and Ijeon(吏典).
July 1447	≪석보상절釋譜詳節≫이 이룩되어 간행. ≪월인천강지곡月印千江之曲≫이 이루어짐. ≪Seokbosangjeol(釋譜詳節)≫ was completed and published. ≪Wolincheongang Jigok(月印千江之曲)≫ was completed.
September 1447	≪동국정운東國正韻≫ 완성. ≪Donggukjjeongun(東國正韻)≫ was completed.
February 1450	왕세자王世子 문종 즉위. The crown prince(王世子) Munjong ascended to the throne.
February 17, 1450	세종대왕이 영응대군永膺大君 집 동별궁東別宮에서 승하함. Sejong the Great passed away at Dongbyulgung Palace(東別宮), the residence of Yeongeungdaegun(永膺大君).

한국어 로마자 표기
Writing Korean in Roman letters

ㄱ					
	가 ga	각 gak	간 gan	갈 gal	감 gam
갑 gap	갓 gat	강 gang	거 geo	건 geon	걸 geol
고 go	곡 gok	곤 gon	골 gol	곳 got	공 gong
곶 got	구 gu	국 guk	군 gun	굴 gul	굿 gut
궁 gung	그 geu	극 geuk	근 geun	글 geul	금 geum
급 geup	긍 geung	기 gi	긴 gin	길 gil	김 gim
개 gae	객 gaek	게 ge	괴 goe	굉 goeng	귀 gwi
겨 gyeo	격 gyeok	견 gyeon	결 gyeol	겸 gyeom	겹 gyeop
경 gyeong	교 gyo	규 gyu	균 gyun	귤 gyul	계 gye
괘 gwae	과 gwa	곽 gwak	관 gwan	괄 gwal	광 gwang
까 kka	꼬 kko	꼭 kkok	꽃 kkot	꾸 kku	꿈 kkum
끝 kkeut	끼 kki	깨 kkae	꾀 kkoe		

ㄴ					
	나 na	낙 nak	난 nan	날 nal	남 nam
납 nap	낭 nang	너 neo	널 neol	노 no	녹 nok
논 non	놀 nol	농 nong	누 nu	눈 nun	눌 nul
느 neu	늑 neuk	늠 neum	능 neung	니 ni	닉 nik
닌 nin	닐 nil	님 nim	내 nae	냉 naeng	네 ne
뇌 noe	녀 nyeo	녁 nyeok	년 nyeon	념 nyeom	녕 nyeong

ㄷ					
	다 da	닥 dak	단 dan	달 dal	담 dam
답 dap	당 dang	더 deo	덕 deok	덜 deol	덤 deom
도 do	독 dok	돈 don	돌 dol	돔 dom	동 dong

두 du	둑 duk	둔 dun	둘 dul	드 deu	득 deuk
들 deul	등 deung	디 di	대 dae	댁 daek	데 de
되 doe	된 doen	뒤 dwi	돼 dwae	따 tta	딱 ttak
또 tto	뚜 ttu	뚝 ttak	뜨 tteu	띠 tti	때 ttae

ㄹ	라 ra	락 rak	란 ran	람 ram	랑 rang
로 ro	록 rok	론 ron	롬 rom	롱 rong	루 ru
르 reu	륵 reuk	른 reun	름 reum	릉 reung	리 ri
린 rin	림 rim	립 rip	링 ring	래 rae	랭 raeng
레 re	렌 ren	뢰 roe	려 ryeo	력 ryeok	련 ryeon
렬 ryeol	렴 ryeom	렵 ryeop	령 ryeong	료 ryo	룡 ryong
류 ryu	륙 ryuk	륜 ryun	률 ryul		

ㅁ	마 ma	막 mak	만 man	말 mal	망 mang
머 meo	먹 meok	모 mo	목 mok	몰 mol	몸 mom
몽 mong	무 mu	묵 muk	문 mun	물 mul	므 meu
미 mi	민 min	밀 mil	매 mae	맥 maek	맨 maen
맹 mang	메 me	뫼 moe	며 myeo	면 myeon	멸 myeol
명 myeong	묘 myo				

ㅂ	바 ba	박 bak	반 ban	발 bal	밤 bam
밥 bap	방 bang	버 beo	번 beon	벌 beol	범 beom
법 beop	보 bo	복 bok	본 bon	봄 bom	봉 bong
부 bu	북 buk	분 bun	불 bul	붐 bum	붕 bung
비 bi	빈 bin	빌 bil	빔 bim	빙 bing	배 bae
백 baek	밴 baen	뱀 baem	뱅 baeng	베 be	벼 byeo
별 byeol	병 byeong	빠 ppa	빵 ppang	뽀 ppo	뿌 ppu
쁘 ppeu	삐 ppi	빼 ppae			

ㅅ

사 sa	삭 sak	산 san	살 sal	삼 sam
삽 sap	상 sang	샅 sat	서 seo	석 seok	선 seon
설 seol	섬 seom	섭 seop	성 seong	소 so	속 sok
손 son	솔 sol	솜 som	솟 sot	송 song	수 su
숙 suk	순 sun	술 sul	숨 sum	숭 sung	숲 sup
스 seu	슬 seul	슴 seum	습 seup	승 seung	시 si
식 sik	신 sin	실 sil	심 sim	십 sip	싱 sing
새 sae	색 saek	샘 saem	생 saeng	세 se	셈 sem
쇄 swae	쉬 swi	쇼 syo	싸 ssa	쏘 sso	쑥 ssak
쓰 sseu	씨 ssi				

ㅇ

아 a	악 ak	안 an	알 al	암 am
압 ap	앙 ang	앞 ap	어 eo	억 eok	언 eon
얼 eol	엄 eom	업 eop	엉 eong	오 o	옥 ok
온 on	올 ol	옴 om	옹 ong	우 u	욱 uk
운 un	울 ul	움 um	웅 ung	으 eu	은 eun
을 eul	음 eum	읍 eup	응 eung	이 i	익 ik
인 in	일 il	임 im	입 ip	잉 ing	애 ae
액 aek	앵 aeng	에 e	외 oe	왼 oen	위 wi
윙 wing	야 ya	약 yak	얀 yan	양 yang	여 yeo
역 yeok	연 yeon	열 yeol	염 yeom	엽 yeop	영 yeong
요 yo	유 yu	육 yuk	윤 yun	율 yul	융 yung
윷 yut	욕 yok	용 yong	의 ui	예 ye	왜 wae
워 wo	원 won	월 wol	와 wa	완 wan	왈 wal
왕 wang					

ㅈ

자 ja	작 jak	잔 jan	잠 jam	잡 jap
장 jang	저 jeo	적 jeok	전 jeon	절 jeol	점 jeom
접 jeop	정 jeong	조 jo	족 jok	존 jon	졸 jol
좀 jom	종 jong	주 ju	죽 juk	준 jun	줄 jul
줌 jum	중 jung	즈 jeu	즉 jeuk	즐 jeul	즘 jeum
즙 jeup	증 jeng	지 ji	직 jik	진 jin	질 jil
짐 jim	집 jip	징 jing	재 jae	잭 jaek	쟁 jaeng
제 je	죄 joe	쥐 jwi	좌 jwa	짜 jja	쪼 jjo
쭈 jju	쭈 jju	쯔 jjeu	찌 jji		

ㅊ

차 cha	착 chak	찬 chan	찰 chal	참 cham
창 chang	처 cheo	척 cheok	천 cheon	철 cheol	첨 cheom
첩 cheop	청 cheong	초 cho	촉 chok	촌 chon	촐 chol
촘 chom	총 chong	추 chu	축 chuk	춘 chun	출 chul
춤 chum	충 chung	측 cheuk	층 cheung	치 chi	칙 chik
침 chim	칩 chip	칭 ching	채 chae	책 chaek	체 che
최 choe	취 chwi				

ㅋ

카 ka	커 keo	코 ko	콩 kong	쿠 ku
쿤 kun	쿨 kul	큰 keun	큼 keum	키 ki	킹 king

ㅌ

타 ta	탁 tak	탄 tan	탈 tal	탐 tam
탑 tap	탕 tang	터 teo	턱 teok	털 teol	토 to
톡 tok	톤 ton	톨 tol	통 tong	투 tu	툭 tuk
툴 tul	퉁 tung	트 teu	특 teuk	튼 teun	틀 teul
틈 teum	티 ti	태 tae	택 taek	탱 taeng	테 te
퇴 toe	튀 twi				

ㅍ	파 pa	팍 pak	판 pan	팔 pal	팜 pam
팡 pang	펌 peom	포 po	폭 pok	폰 pon	퐁 pong
푸 pu	푹 puk	품 pum	풍 pung	프 peu	피 pi
픽 pik	핀 pin	필 pil	핍 pip	패 pae	팽 paeng
페 pe	펜 pen	펴 pyeo	편 pyeon	폄 pyeom	평 pyeung
표 pyo					

ㅎ	하 ha	학 hak	한 han	할 hal	함 ham
합 hap	항 hang	허 heo	헉 heok	헌 heon	험 heom
헝 heong	호 ho	혹 gok	혼 hon	홀 hol	홈 hom
홉 hop	홍 hong	후 hu	훅 huk	훈 hun	훔 hum
훙 hung	흐 heu	흑 heuk	흔 heun	흠 heum	흥 heung
히 hi	힘 him	해 hae	핵 haek	햄 haem	행 haeng
헤 he	회 hoe	획 hoek	횡 hoeng	휘 hwi	혀 hyeo
혁 hyeok	현 hyeon	혈 hyeol	혐 hyeom	형 hyeong	효 hyo
휴 hyu	휼 hyul	흉 hyung	홰 hwae	횃 hwaet	훼 hwe
훤 hwon	화 hwa	확 hwak	환 hwan	활 hwal	황 hwang